T0114058

125 Poems with Rhyme

Phillip Batesole

ISBN: 978-1-4120-4393-9 (sc)

Trafford rev. 11/28/2019

www.trafford.com

North America & international
toll-free: 1 888 232 4444 (USA & Canada)
fax: 812 355 4082

Foreword

Hi my name is Phil Batesole
the author of this book.
I grew up in Fremont, Ohio
and have lived there most
of my life. In the Spring
of 2002 I began writing this
book of rhyming poetry.
I was first inspired by
listening to music but I
love poetry of all kinds
and I hope you find it a
good read. Thank You.

Table of Contents

One Hundred and Twenty Five Poems with Rhyme
By Phil Batesole

One Hundred American Poems

I am proud to be an American
America is what I know
Fish, fowl or game
You'll always know the wild
And the tame in America
The home of the free and the brave

A Poem to be Remembered

A poem to be remembered
A light snowy day in November
A cucumber salad for dinner
An old musical ballad
The Winter's Dawn

A Day in June

A Day in June
The color blue
Everybody plays the fool
Almost drown in the pool
A day in June
The man always had a tool
The man in the moon
The name of the tune
A Day in June

The Beautiful Blonde

The beautiful blonde
The woman with the wand
The beautiful blonde
The bosom of the hon
The beautiful blonde
The man was a con
The beautiful blonde

Hi's and Goodbyes

Hi's and goodbyes
Everything's all right
If you're here tonight
Hi's and goodbyes
Hope you're feeling fine
Thought I'd leave this behind
Hi's and goodbyes

The Beautiful Girl

She looked a mess in the tattered dress
Though she was still a beautiful tess
She didn't know ole Mo
But she knew little Andrew
And how she still somehow shined through
If I knew then what I know now
I would have been proud to ask her out

Another Rhyme

Tried hard to play ball
Took my best girl to the mall
Voices coming from down the hall
If you heard one you heard them all
Not so true though
If you know her still
Put her in your will
For she was the one with looks that could kill

World Wars

World Wars
Oh my gosh what for
Nazi abuse
What is the use
The Gestapo
How unheartful
The painful wounds
The mourning sounds
World war what for
Make amends
Hope the war ends
World Wars

The Dinner

Wine and Dine
Oh so fine
Wine and Dine
Almost all the time
Wine and Dine
Stop on a dime
Wine and Dine
The end of time
Wine and Dine
Oh so fine
Wine and Dine

Phillip Batesole

A Week in the Past

Puns on Monday
Dues on Tuesday
Amends on Wednesday
Cruise on Thursday
Fried Fish on Friday
Matters on Saturday
Gracefulness on Sunday

10

Karate Practice

Karate Practice
Sweat and Malice
Karate Practice
Punch and Kick
Karate Practice
Wunch and Wick
Karate Practice
How much do you want it
Karate Practice

Phil's Will

Phil's Will
Phil has a will
Phil's Will
The Farmer in the Dell
Phil's Will
Started to Swell
Phil's Will
Ring my Bell
Ring my Bell
Ring my Bell

Only the Good Lord Knows

Soldiers and Saints
And 50 cent rates
Martyrs and Members
Oh how I Remember
The Sweat and the Grit
And the Whole Total Whit
How it comes and goes
The Rain and the Snow
And as the Wind Blows
Only the Good Lord Knows

A Mother's

A Mother is always kind
She never upsets her child's mind
A Mother always shares her time
She is always oh so fine
A Mother always finds the time

A Friend's

A friend is always there
A friend always cares
A friend always shares
A friend has the time
A friend on my mind
A friend is always kind

Phillip Batesole

A Poem For My Dad

Donald my Dad
What a Fad
Not a good Lad
Do not be Mad
I Love my Dad
Hope you're never sad
I was sometimes bad
I'm a Lad
I am my Dad

For Ronald My Friend

Ronald a man
No not a can of beer
No not a man of fear
He'll be your fan
If you're in the band
Just lend a hand

Mental Health

Mental Health
Wonders Wealth
Mental Health
Plunder's Melt
Mental Health
Practice Stealth
Mental Health
Heaven and Hell
Mental Health

Beautiful for Beverly

Beautiful flowers on the avenue
Oh how I love you
If I were a flower I'd be a flower for you
The color blue
The blue skies above
Your skin as soft as a dove's wings
I once brought you wild thing
Oh seamore
For my wife I now long for ever more

Phillip Batesole

Autumn's Hope

A salt mine in my nose
Wouldn't you know it
It is autumn again and
I got a cold
Won't be long now
Santa be back around
Shooting over the mountains
Flowing with the clouds

How Would it go Down

Rust, yellow, red and brown
If you were arrested
How would it go down
Would you cry with the
Tears of a clown
Or would you be glad to be mad
And be terribly sad
However it might go down
Definitely with a frown

The Ugs

A bug in the rug
A rub in the tub
A hug in the pub
A snug in the hub
A mug in the cub

Hickory Dickory Dock

Hickory Dickory Dock
The mouse climbed up the clock
The clock struck one
The mouse fell on
Hickory Dickory Dock

Phillip Batesole

The Air Above and the Earth Below

The air is light
The total height
The heavens above
The pure white snow
The earth below
The Miracles

The Game 1

The face of a man
The shout of the fans
The sound of the band
The pace of a man
The race and the fans
The outcome in the end

The Hare and the Wren

The hare and the wren
The large hare
The small wren
The catch in a snare
The bird much smaller than a hen
The hare in his den
The wren in his nest
The best of the best
The hare and the wren

The Prince and the Princess

The brave knight
Did his best
Was put to the test
The beautiful princess
With beautiful long hair
Put into require
Both together
Made the fire
And forever
Remained together

The Wisdom of God

The wisdom of God
All the true words
All the unremorse
All of the whole universe
Not a curse but a blessing
The wisdom of God

A Rhyme

Ride Sally ride
High in the sky
Let it ride
Bachman Turner Overdrive
The king is still alive
Rock and Roll will never die

A Tale

The Apples
The Snapples
The Cranberries
The Shady Ole Shanties
The Spanish Moss
The Ole Man Hoss
The Smae Ole Boss
The Ole Rugged Cross

The Cat's Meow

The Old Lion
The Mellow Yellow
The Mild tame one
The Cat's Meow
The big cat the small cat
The furballs and shampoo
The other cat's meow
The Young Lion

Ben and Ken

Ben and Ken
If Ben wasn't a friend
Ben and Ken
The can is in the sack
Ben and Ken
Out to MacDonald's
Ben and Ken
For a Big Mac
Ben and Ken
Or if Ken was your friend
Ben and Ken
Who would you be ole man

The Truth

The Adventure of Life is to Learn
The Purpose of Life is to Grow
The Nature of Life is to Change
The Essence of Life is to Care
The Challenge of Life is to Overcome

Once Upon a Time

Once upon a Time
The Rhythm and the Rhyme
A Poem that Rhymes
With a message for the time
The Rhythm and the rhyme
Poems with few or many lines
All at the right time
Once upon a Time

The Four Elements

The Maken by God
In the right mood
From earth came the birth
The Waters the mirth
The Air so fair
The Fire and the nightmares
The Earth
The Water
The Air
The Fire

Phillip Batesole

A 9th Grade Poem

```
            V
            E
            R
            T
HORIZONTAL
            C
            A
            L
```

36

Love is the Only Way

Love is the only way
For the sake of the little babies
For the heavenly way of the elderly
Love is the only way
For the hope that brings tomorrow
For the ole ride in the wheelbarrow
Love is the only way
For the sunny days
For the rainy days
Love is the only way

Phillip Batesole

Moses and the Red Roses

Moses and the Red Roses
Hoses for the noses
Pleasing the many noses
A picture to the eyes
As cold as the ice
The doans for the moans and groans
Thanks for the many loans
Hope I repay in full
Let the Red Roses Flow
Moses and the Red Roses

In My Eyes

In my eyes
Tiny Bubbles
In my eyes
Zesty Pests
In my eyes
Snarling pain
In my eyes
Rinse please
In my eyes
I don't need these
In my eyes

Phillip Batesole

The Time

The Reason for the Season
The Teasing for the Pleasing
The Love of the Dove
Above all time
And past the line
The Time

A Painter a Poet

A Painter a Poet
A Fainter a Foe at
If I knew it I would know it
The Life grew
I knew it
To be or not to be
Reality
A Fainter a foe at
A Painter a poet

Not In Vain

For to be or not to be
Be it the death of a flea
Not the death of millions
Not in Vain

One to Ten

One Two live it through
Three Four never ignore
Five Six Truths and Myths
Seven Eight never be late
Nine Ten do it all again

One to Twelve

One Two buckle your shoe
Three Four open the door
Five Six potato sticks
Seven Eight don't be late
Nine Ten do it again
Eleven Twelve help the Elves

The Stallion and the Hare

The Stallion stood with a stare
The Hare ran the way he would
The Mare saw the Stallion and knew he could
The Hare was on his way and would
And they all roamed through the night
Until the morning light

Phillip Batesole

The Red White and Blue

The Red White and Blue
Whether I'm in good health
Or I got the flu
I salute the Red White and Blue
Always to be true
To the Red White and Blue
Whether I'm at work or at school
I salute the Red White and Blue
As an American not as a fool
The Red White and Blue

A Clown

A clown without a frown
A clown always around
A clown without a town
A clown always known
A clown with a hound
A clown that was bound
A clown without a sound

Kitty Kats and Straw Hats

Kitty Kats and straw hats
How do you this
How do you that
The boy up to bat
The old firehouse and the bats
The best way to do this
The best way to do that
Kitty Kats and straw hats

Farah Jocha

Farah-Jocha-Farah-Jocha
Cars and trucks
A roaming rack of ruck
Trains and planes
All kinds of things
Farah-Jocha-Farah-Jocha

This Land We Know

Wide open spaces where the buffalo roam
Clear prairie plains we can call our home
High snow-peaked mountains all filled with gnomes
Know where on earth that needs to moan
Careful now we don't need any broken bones
High or low warm or cold this land is our own

A Message From the Past

Once upon a time there was a man
His sadness about drove him mad
When he was a lad he was sometimes bad
He simply didn't know what they had
Still willed the ill to be gone
It was almost over and he was done
The lad then went up the road
Over and abroad to the hill
Laid down and stayed quite still
Then he took hold for a look
As he took the road north
He ended forth and last
And it all now is in the past

Phillip Batesole

The Halls

I walked down the hall
Someone called my name
Back then fame was
The name of the game
It was almost always the same
After the fall
We went to the mall
Drank coffee and had a ball
I walked down the hall

Pieces of the Past

Went to a party last night
Smoked some grass with fright
Have got the cash
Just ask Nash
For the Hash
It is a must
And this is a bust
Going fishing for bass
All somewhere in my past

Family and the Holidays

Dirky and Dougy
A smile and a huggy
Wood sittin' in a tree
A dog with fleas
A long time ago
Just across the road
The seasons come and go
What did you know
We all hope it snows

Fame

The man played for fame
That was the name of the game
The man then fell for the dame
There was no-one to blame
The woman was forever his flame
The man played for fame

A Day in May

We took a ride across the bay
It was a day in May
We picnicked all day
It was a real roll in the hay
We wished for a longer stay
We watched the sun go down as we laid

An Empty Night

It was three on one
They had their buck-knife and gun
And it all was not much fun
And it was done and I was done
With the empty enemy's gun

Phillip Batesole

Together at Home

As we sat at home
The evening was aglow
It was after a fall
And after all
It was after a fall
We were in love
With the flight of the dove
It could have been a romantic cove
But it wasn't it was simple
And my wife has cute dimples
As we sat at home

Many with Rhyme

Time and Rhyme
Lemon and lime
It's summertime
Again a line
Twice with Chimes
Once with time
Many with rhyme
Many with rhyme
Once with time
Twice with chimes
Again a line
It is winter time
Tea will be fine
Rhyme many a time

Phillip Batesole

The Game 2

Playing football
In for the long haul
Playing with the big boys
Buying the little ones toys
Doing what you're supposed to do
Playing the tough kind of game
That is the total call for the game

The Green Grass

As the green grass grows
As the cold wind blows
As everything I've known
The cold has blown the snow
As everything I know
The green grass will still grow

Phillip Batesole

Weathering the Storm

Weathering the storm
Staying safe and warm for now
Making sure none of us come to harm
The strong winds the norm
Praying for the safety of others
Mothers, Sisters, Fathers and Brothers
Married couples and others
Weathering the storm

The Right Choice

If it is the booze you choose
You're sure to be the one that will lose
Take it from me then if you will
Choose not the booze to lose
But the right to choose the way you will
It takes more than one leg to climb the hill
And I hope you choose the right will

Phillip Batesole

The Extra Cash

A broken head a tortured tail
I hope not to fail
For a tale to be told
For I am getting old
For when I rise in the morning
The first thing I think is boring
It is lighting up the little turd burling
And adding a little turdling ash
Sometimes we all need the extra cash

A December to be Remembered

A December to remember
Whether transient or member
It will be a December to remember
Whether a Santa or a Reindeer
It will be a December to remember
Whether rich child or poor child
It will be a December to remember
Whether gift or gifts
It will be a December to be Remembered

Phillip Batesole

Another Poem

The Oceans and the Seas
The Rivers and the Streams
The man named Hercules
The city named Rome
The caves and the gnomes
The old man's home
Another Poem

The Body and the Blood

The Body and the Blood
The thick and the thin
The within and the without
The Body of the Host
The Blood thicker than the water
The Lord of Hosts
The God from Above
The Body and the Blood

Phillip Batesole

The Couch or the Kangaroo

Like an old dacron couch
Like a kangaroo in the zoo
The kangaroo in the zoo
The kangaroo has a pouch
The couch has honor and comfort for you
With both the couch or the kangaroo
You can either rest or go to the zoo

Hot Wheels

Hot Wheels and their track
Racing back to back
The Hot Wheels shooting through
The Hot Wheels house
Whether they're red, yellow, pink or blue
They're always fun to play with too

The live and let live

To be or not to be
These words in history
Whether me or you
They are in the world
To live or to die
Or to commit suicide
William Shakespeare in a play
Be it you or be it me
I truly believe he would say
If he were alive today
Live and let live

The Fat Rat and the Man

The fat rat sat
As the fat rat sat he said
Look look at that
The man stopped in his tracks
The man then said
What is That! That!
The fat rat then replied
It is what it is

Phillip Batesole

Flowers and Weeds

The Oceans and Seas
The Birds and the Bees
The flowers and the trees
The rivers and the streams
Flowers are still better than weeds

The Deer

Doe a Deer
A female deer
A Roe
A Roaming
Rack of Ruck
A buck

Phillip Batesole

A Ying for the Yang

A Ying for the Yang
A won for the win
A Ying for the Yang
A hon for the hin
A Ying for the Yang
A done for the din
A Ying for the Yang
A pawn for the pin
A Ying for the Yang
A yawn for the yin
A Wing for the Yang

A PRAYER

Birds of a feather flock together
Fish in water swim and wander
Man and Woman live together
And all is one forever and ever
Amen...

Never Misunderstood

If I had to be bad
It would be nad
If I had to be good
It would be wood
If I had to be mad
It would be bad
And if I understood
It would and could
Never misunderstood

Ole King Cole

Ole King Cole was a merry ole soul
A merry ole soul he was
He'd drink his rum and smoke his pipe
And sleep a king all through the night
In the morning he would rise
And with great surprise
He would rise

Phillip Batesole

The Three

With wisdom, spirit and soul
They all still seem to come and go
With Rock and Roll in their hearts
With all the burps and farts
As they said in the days of old
The show must go on
Phil and Don and brother Michael

Squirming Like a Toad

Squirming like a Toad
Riding down tobacco road
A truck pulling a heavy load
Not knowing which way to go
Slow as she goes
Bow over the stern
Going with the flow
We'll know where to go
Weathering the storm
Whether blowing smoke
Or burning up the road
Squirming like a toad

Dear old Dad

Dear old Dad
Sometimes got mad
Although he was never bad
That I knew
Now that he has grown old
God please bless his soul
Dear old Dad

The Reunions

The horse the deer
The boredom the beer
Myself and my dear
The hype and the fear
God bless and take care
See ya in five years

Phillip Batesole

Catch me if you can

Not having a very good day
Trying to get along with it anyway
Guess I'll write another one
I'll try anyway for now
A Howdy Doo a Howdy How
Well try later then
And make some amends
Catch me if you can

For the Poem

Writing another poem
Like Sly and the Family Stone
Or Mark Cohn
Doing what is right
And never being wrong
Playing the old song
For the poem

Here I am

There they go
The War's on
The war was over
On up to the north
Yes-no
Here I go
There I went
Here I am
When will it end
Never they said
Well it was over
The War's on
There they go
Here I am

Sing a Song

Sing a song
If it is soft or loud
Sing along
Learning how to play
Sing along
O yes anyway you choose
O yes anyway you choose
Sing along
Play it yes
Sing it soft or loud
Sing along
Learn how to play
Sing along

Rhythm and Rhyme

Rhythm and Rhyme
O what a time
Will I survive
Rhythm and Rhyme
Always in my mind
A good feeling
Like sweet sunshine
O what a time
I will survive
Rhythm and Rhyme

Hope

Here another line for a poem
The cats outside in the cold
One light One Dark both bold
If I can keep them tame I will
But if I can't, they will still grow old
This is just another poem
Hope they all come home

Phillip Batesole

Riding Down the Highway

Riding down the highway
Going back to your hideaway
Riding down the highway
The music can never be too loud
Going down the road in your car
You can never be too proud
Riding down the highway
Going back to your hideaway
I don't want to say goodbye
All I want to do is say Hi
Are you going my way
Riding down the highway
Going back to your hideaway

The Cat's Meow

The Old Lion
The Mellow Yellow
The Mild Tame One
The Cat's Meow
The big cat the small cat
The furballs and shampoo
The Cat's Meow

Scott, Eric and I

Scott, Eric and I
If I thought I could fly
I'd be high in the sky
The pot the beer the guys
I can't be you
I can only be I
Scott the beer
And Eric the bright
Scott, Eric and I

That I Knew

That I knew
The cold snow blew
The kind wind was cold
As bold as cold and old
I knew but never wept
The attempt would fail
And was kept in full
Till the spring
And then it would ring new
That I knew

I'll Be Kind

I'll be kind
I was a baby long ago
No baby Huey was I though
Not born deaf or blind
You can read my mind
Sorry next time
I'll be kind

The Tale of Two

Once upon a time
There was a man
With a bottle of wine
This man said
If I only had a load of bread
I would be a happier lad
So the man went to the store
Which was not very far
The man bought the loaf of bread
And the said
I am a happier lad
Now I have a bottle of wine
And now I have a loaf of bread
And the man ate and drank
Until the bread and wine were gone
And now this poem is done

Phillip Batesole

Let's See

Let's see
What is there left
For you and me
The shifting seas
The bellowing winds
The getting down on your knees
The getting down on your knees
The bellowing winds
The shifting seas
For you and me
What is there left
Let's see

Life and a Friend

Heaven's above Hell's below
Go with the dove go with the flow
Life is short but life is a miracle
If you know me now you will know me then
Hope to meet you then as a friend
From the beginning to the end
Heaven's above Hell's below

From Beginning to End

Space and Time
Fruit of the Vine
Rhythm and Rhyme
A mountain to climb
A sky to fly
An ocean to swim
If I were you
And you were him
From bow to stern
Hope all will learn

The Newspaper Press

The Newspaper Press
The Interesting Messes
Putting in the Presses
The Paper and Inks
And Messages of Who's Right
And Who Stinks
The Reporter's Stories
And the Poet's Poems
Who's Right and Who's Wrong
The Newspaper Press

Phillip Batesole

The Grocery Store

Going in the automatic doors
Finding the right cart
Just as you start
The filing in of items
The checkout line
The checks or cash
You're out of the store
And finished at last

The Date

I took her out on a date
We went out and ate
I brought her home it was late
I was sure she would make
The right mate
It was her birthday
I baked her a cake
And we took the day
And went to the lake
It was a great day we would make

A Girl called Daisy

Her name was Daisy
And he was often lazy
She probably thought
He was crazy
He played Purple Haze
Like mice in a maze
And added a phrase
Her name was Daisy
And they often played
Nearly everyday
He spoke her name

People and Me

On the bed not in the washer
Take them off just give them a toss
Out of the washer into the dryer
My mother's maiden name was Meyer
Homosapiens are people not things
Although I was once a hobo ming
And I lived in missions and used to sing
Life goes on for everyone
If they can believe in everything

Birds of the Air

Birds of the air
Birds of a feather
Birds a mourning dove
Birds of the lord above
Birds of earth's nectar
Birds in a nest together
Birds of a feather
Birds of the air

Mr. J. and Mr. P.

Mr. Jingles
Jingle Jangle
Mr. Pringles
Munch and Mingle
If a mouse
Mr. Jingles
If a chip
Mr. Pringles

Elements

Air we breathe
Water we need
Earth we sow
Fire we light and put out
Thanks and praise
We give with grace
Man at his best pace
In the human race

Life is short
Let us come to rest
Before we go to
Remain with
The Lord

Painters and Poets

Painters and Poets
People who do know it
Memories and Moments
People who do not know it
Memories and Moments
All who do and do not know it
Painters and Poets

The Lady and the Man

The lady looked pretty in pink
In her stole made of soft mink
She passed the man and gave a wink
The man reached down and grabbed his dink
The man was definitely too kinky
And the woman meek in her mink
Anyway I hope this poem didn't make a big stink

The Date

You got a date
Don't be late
Might be your next mate
I hope it don't turn to hate
If it is a long line
You might have to wait
Next time go first rate

Orville and Wilbur Wright

Orville and Wilbur Wright
One hundred years of Flight
Wheels on the ground
Yes we are going to be skybound
When the sun is full of delight
Or the moon is aglow at night
Hope nothing becomes a fright
One hundred years of flight
Orville and Wilbur Wright

Phillip Batesole

Days and Nights

Days and Nights of old
Friday night at the flights
Saturdays with old head lights
Sundays with Jesus Christ
Monday afternoons in the park
Tuesdays listening to the dogs bark
Darkness he called night
Light he called day
Wednesday a moonlit night
Thursday a day to be bright

110

One to Twelve again

One for the Hon
Two for the Mule
Three for the Degrees
Four for the floor
Five for the Dive
Six for the Pixee Stix
Seven for the Eleven
Eight for the Straight
Nine for the Pine
Ten for the Men
Eleven for the Heaven
Twelve for the Elves

The Man

I loved the man
Did you know Uncle Dan
We were all his fans
Even Matthew his son
Gone now sorry to say
He once had a roll
In the Hay
That I'm not sorry to say
I loved the man

Ode to Morris

Phil is getting Fat
You don't need that
Time to slim down
Not to whine like a hound
And not again bound
But to love everything you have
Like that
Phil is getting Fat

Phillip Batesole

Buds and Duds

A Bud and new Duds
Like Bugs Bunny and Elmer Fudd
Whether the Gap at the mall
Or at the Plaza at Goodwill
You will find Duds still
And at the bar the Bud
Will be suds for goodwill
A Bud and new Duds

My Wife

The more I think of her
The more I love her
If I thought of her once
I thought of her twice
Yes even thrice and quatro
Married her forever
Always to remember
Yes even in the middle of September
Or the middle of May
The more I love her
The more I think of her

Reality

I sat on the floor
They walked through the door
There were four
The rain would pour
And the taste was sour
But I did not ignore
I sat on the floor

Purple Power

The Purple Flower
Held the Power
The Fans that Wow'ers
Held the Power
The Purple Flower
Purple Power

Phillip Batesole

Seven Cups of Coffee

Seven cups of coffee
Seven cups of coffee
Eleven pints of gold
Eleven pints of gold
O now what don't you know
O now what don't you know

Times

Happy Times
Sad Times
Good Times
Bad Times
Present Times
Past Times
Fast Times
Slow Times
Future Times
Nurture Times

Phillip Batesole

A Prayer

As I lay me down to sleep
I pray the lord my soul to keep
For if I die before I awake
I know I will rest in eternal sleep

Sleepless Nights

All the sleepless nights
Some filled with fright
For to live is for Christ
And to die is gain
I know somewhere I'll remain
And a night's peace
I will attain

Do It Right

Try never to be uptight
Be bright and full of light
Try to keep things insight
Everything should be alright
Hope nothing turns a fright
Guess I'll go the extra mile
Then glide for awhile
Until the feeling's right
So don't be uptight
Do it right

My Wife and I

I would care for her
And she would care for me
I would continue writing
And she would continue dieting
I would sometimes stare at her
And she would glare back at me
I knew she loved me
And I knew I loved her
Now until forever

From Me To You

The tobacco you smoke
The cigarettes you toke
The coffee you drink
The toffee you chew
The cats you feed
The dogs you bathe
The money you need
The honey you eat

125

Black is Beautiful
White is Wonderful
Phil got the Hill
Phil was always on the Dill
Friend or Foe
Buck or Doe
A man named Phil or Edgar Allen Poe
You Choose You
Who will win or lose

Printed in the United States
By Bookmasters